A Poet's Playground

Cheydrea

A Poet's Playground is raw, vulnerable and savage.

It includes poetry, artwork, personal quotes and short personal stories written in the midst of a painful and unexpected inner child healing period.

The painted pages reveal how my inner child found her bypassed and buried wounds, how she discovered her voice through writing, and how two decades of depression and grief turned into a life saving human transformation. It took incredible courage and strength for me to fall off the ledge, piece my angst back together, and share it with anyone who is meant to find it.

My sincerest hope is that A Poet's Playground will transmute your emotional pain into clarity, self-understanding, self-compassion, self-trust, and a strong dose of HOPE.

Authenticity

honest, raw
full of emotion,
human expression

to feel

Contents

@Cheydrea

Please share my pen name **@Cheydrea** when
sharing and using my poetry and quotes,
and please tag me.

I will try to say hello when you do.

I am grateful for your support, beyond
measure because everyone deserves support.

If you are from a broken home, I hope my
words help you feel understood, and I hope
you will feel inspired to write or paint or
whatever helps you breathe.

savage [sav-ij]

instinctual; ██████ primitive; wild; brave; █████ exotic; ██████ primal; ██████ raw; ██████ unapologetic; tough; ██████ unsuppressed; free; unfiltered;

Poetry is...

Purging.

Extractions of long- winded written emotional exhales.

The art of self-expression.

Bravely feeling, while painting a messy canvas of angst and hope.

Promises to ourselves.

Saving a life.

Validation for others.

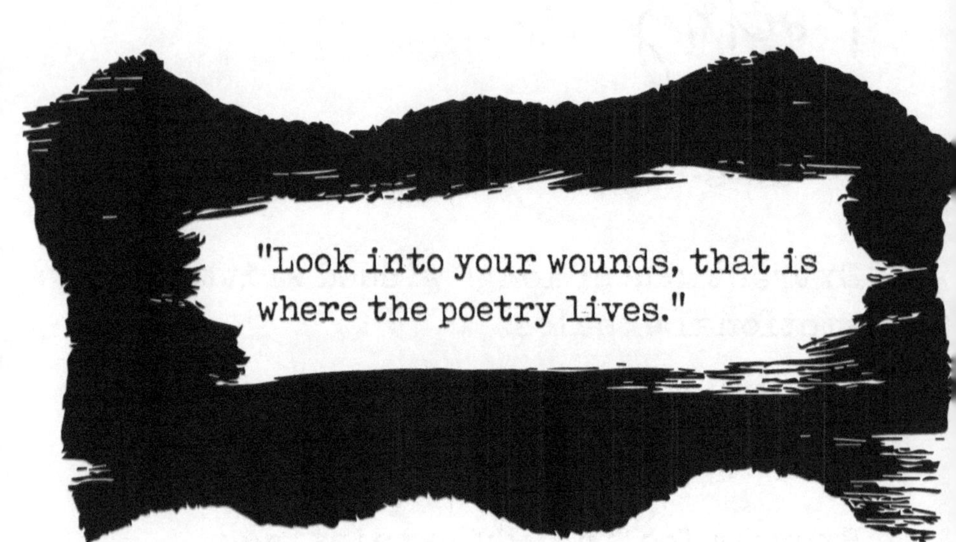

"Look into your wounds, that is where the poetry lives."

 I was exhausted and weary,
tired of abandoning myself –
tired of hiding my depression
and grief. Tired of keeping it
all together, aiming for
perfection and the desire to please.

I took a few years to really focus on
my healing. To face my wounds and stop
bypassing the pain that was slowly
suffocating my beautiful joyful spirit.

It hasn't come without great sacrifice
or daring to be misunderstood. I may be
judged and criticized but I vow to
never abandon my heart, my voice, or my
inner child – ever again!

She was waiting for me, so I showed the
fuck up. Caution! I am savage with my
words.

Healing

To face and honor one's wounds; to remember; to grieve; to feel and to unapologetically express a full spectrum of human emotions; to nurture; to embody compassion.

Anyone can play on the

poet's playground, but there is one
very important rule...You must dare to
feel and dare to express yourself.

If you are in anguish, be a poet.
You don't have to stay a poet.
You don't have to stay anything.

You can change your mind,
and BE who you need to be,
for the time it takes,
to become you again.

If you don't want to be a poet,
sing...write...paint...dance...
the voice of your wounds and the truth
of your beautiful scars.

Feelings

Feelings are like barbed wire;
they will tear your flesh into
ribbons.

I promise you won't bleed to death.
 - if you are determined to heal
and express yourself.

Every Poet

The following page is my BURN
page.

Because every poet burns it down.

Because foundations erode
and structures need rebuilding.

Burn it down to ashes.

The judgement

The ignorance

The lies

The brainwashing

The betrayal

The rejection

The jealousy

The perfectionism

The hate

The shame

The distractions

The hypocrisy

The evil

The greed

The gluttony

The fear

We must BURN it all down if we ever
Hope to RISE.

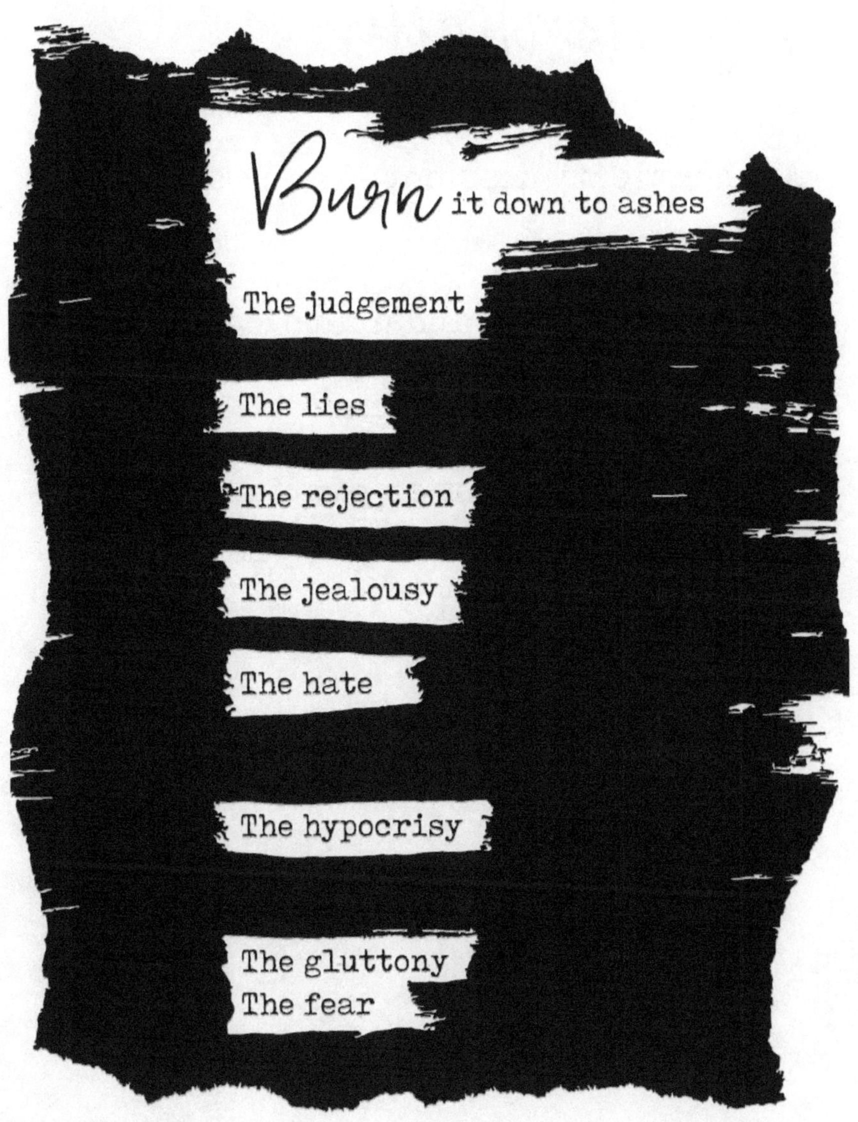
Burn it down to ashes

The judgement

The lies

The rejection

The jealousy

The hate

The hypocrisy

The gluttony
The fear

Authenticity

Authenticity does not play it safe or sweet.

It is honest, raw and unapologetic.

It is full of expression.

It weaves every human emotion into a magnificent tapestry of what it truly means to feel.

I ~~have~~ *had a* Disease.

the "disease to please."

I am a recovering perfectionist.
A recovering people pleaser. An
empty and eroding well, always
giving without asking or
expecting anything in return.

In my family of origin, I learned
this was the only way to survive
in order to belong.

I was abandoned and neglected as a
child. There was also abuse. This
is where my disease began.
Scripture fed the lonely beast.
Learning and naming these truths
was the lifeblood of my recovery
from this disease, and my unhealed
perpetual grief.

If there was a place we could go, and sit in a circle, and talk about all the things we've done to please and pour into others, I would be in that circle.

"The People Pleasers Circle"

We would meet daily, because once a week wouldn't be enough. There would be a line around the block to get in. I imagine thousands of women. Some men too. Every shape and color. Every culture.

Maybe this circle would be better titled "Perfectionists Anonymous," except we wouldn't be anonymous. We would stand up and shout in anger, sing without mercy, dance unclothed, and celebrate.

"Our songs and our clamors would repair our eroding wells and fill them up with the water from our endless tears. They would overflow into rivers of love for humanity."

Cheers

to all the recovering perfectionists and people pleasers. Do yourself a generous favor and make a huge mess of things for a while. Carry no shame or guilt and make no apologies as you untangle the mess in search of your authentic self.

Then pick yourself up and put all the pieces back together again. Not the old and familiar pieces. The unrecognizable pieces. The beautiful and wonderful pieces that you lost along the way.

Take all the time you need.

Frozen Tears

I dream of reaching the top of the
mountain I've been climbing.

My hands calloused,

clinging, forging, anchoring.

My tears frozen,

to my skin of ice.

My mind weary,

and bones aching.

My heart bleeds,

as I forfeit my old self,

by exhaustion.

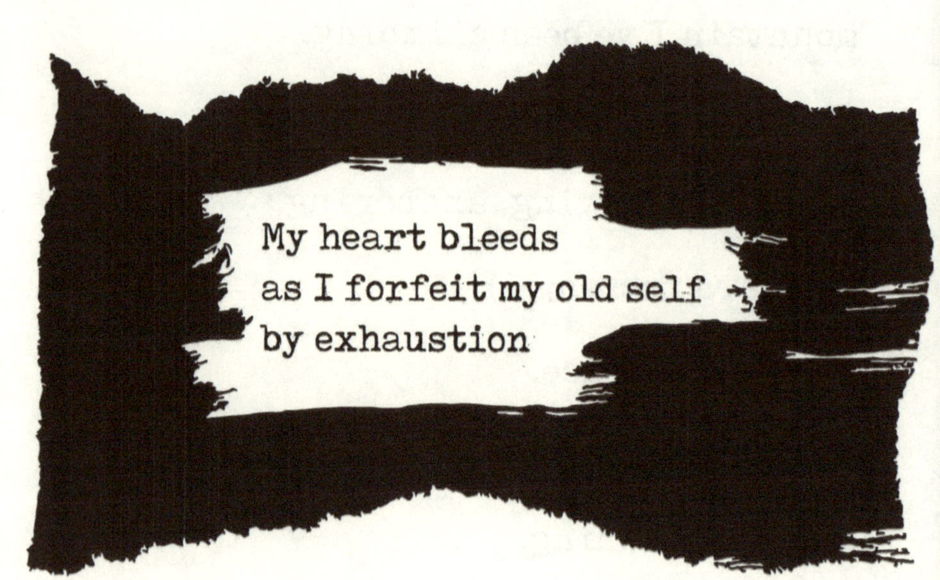
My heart bleeds
as I forfeit my old self
by exhaustion

Angels

Angels hold space for those who must
heal.

The angel of self-compassion
lives inside of us.

She is the most powerful angel of
all.

Love

Love doesn't lie.

Love never abandons.

Love doesn't excuse or refute.

Love is not silent or cold.

Love does not shame or bully.

Love supports.

Love tries.

Love sees.

Love feels.

Love holds.

Love heals.

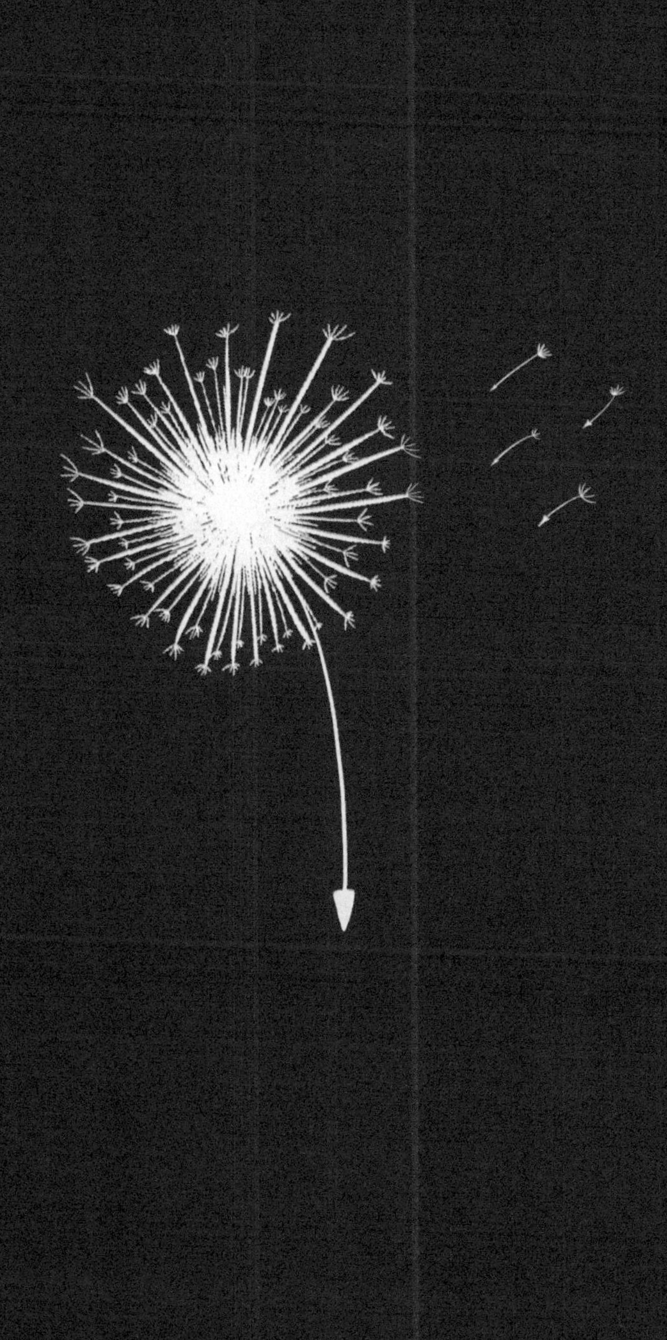

Savage

I'm not a conformist. I'm
an intuitive rebel and **savage cycle
breaker**, who's not afraid of
sacrifice.

I never wanted to be a cycle breaker, I wanted to belong.

There is always a cost to belonging, and I wasn't able or willing to pay the price.

Honor thy Soul

I needed to move away to a new place, to leave my native state and family – and become who I needed to become. I had to recapture the lost parts of my soul.

This means giving up everything you've ever known in hopes for something your heart can only imagine. It means unimaginable loneliness, uncertainty, and waves of regret.

It means losing so you can win, so that you can protect everything that is sacred to you. It costs you everything, but you gain so much more. You shed, you peel, you ache, you bleed and then you stitch yourself together, thread by thread.

You begin to discover yourself.
Not in a day or a year, but in
decades.

Breaking cycles is lonely. The
grief persists, like some sort of
intermittent torture ritual, but
your soul is the sage - it keeps
reminding you why. It is the
gatekeeper.

With time and blistering
intention, you don't succumb to
inauthentic circles or mind-
numbing activities. You endure
all that continues to come -
sorrow, self-doubt, and fear.

You stay, you listen, and you
follow the promise of your soul.

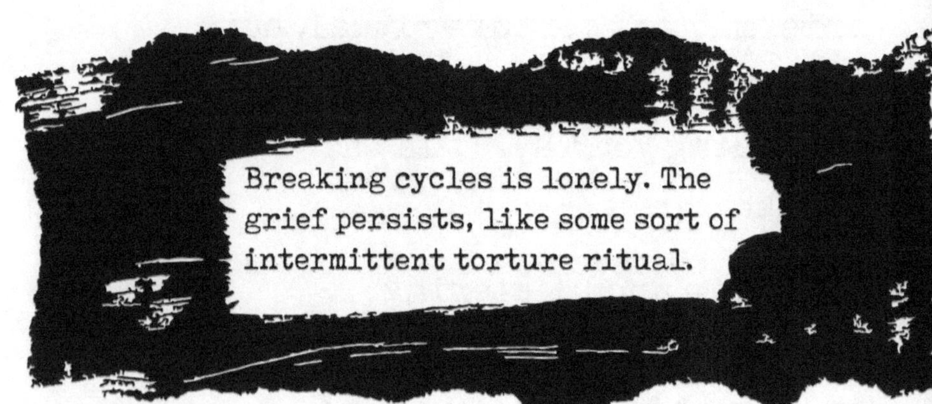
Breaking cycles is lonely. The
grief persists, like some sort of
intermittent torture ritual.

Ugly Places

I'm sorry dear one,
if you want to extract the venom
from your veins, you have to return to
the ugly places where it
all began.

Bring self-compassion with you.
Keep it close. Strap it to your
heart.

It's a fierce tool that skillful
warriors use - to slay the
vampires who drink from your
magnificent soul.

The soul knows

It is quiet,

it listens,

it waits.

It is skillful,

magnificent,

intuitive.

It is fierce,

resilient,

fire.

It is Savage

Reclaim your spirit.

Reclaim your power.
When someone rejects your experiences and your feelings it takes your power away. It adds poison to your wounds and prevents healing. It strangles your throat, and you lose your voice.

Invite your emotions in. Give written words to your fears, your grief, your anger, your memories.

Nurture and hold yourself without hate, shame, or judgement – until you find the courage to express yourself.

Use your voice to support your healing and reclaim your power.

Reclaim your voice.
Reclaim your spirit.
Reclaim your power.

Perfection

Perfection is a shovel for your grave. It is self-abuse.

I know you were hoping they would
cherish you someday.

Wishing for them to understand
you, longing for their presence to
dissolve your grief.

Believing if you were
pretty enough,
smart enough,
kind enough,
good enough,
patient enough,
performing and pleasing enough,
religious and prayerful enough,
hard working enough,
that someday maybe,
you would be enough!

A rare diamond you were, but all you saw was the mud and the dirt, layer upon layer.

You carried your heavy shovel, pushing and digging, exhausting yourself to the point of no return.

Finally realizing you were more than enough, you set down your shovel, traded it for a shield & sword, and you walked away.

Those Who Love

Those who know what love is will do whatever it takes to fix the things that break the ones they say they love.

Don't
abandon
~~family~~ yourself!

Purging

Purging releases trauma
from your bones
your organs
your mind.

Write it. Name it.
Paint it. Color it.
Sing it. Pitch it.
Dance it. Release it.
Scream it. Heave it.
Heal it and Rise!

Writing saved me,
after it flayed me.

Words

Words are like poison – they eat
away at the spirit.

They lose their power when you
name them and extract the poison
over and over again.

Every time I read these pages, it
hurts less and less.

Like fire turned to cold ashes
that have blown away in the wind.

Let their chaos and constant distractions motivate your presence and inner calm.

Projections

Other people's "internal world"
projected onto you – to create
chaos in your mind and break your
heart open – time and time again.

Projections will chronically
confuse and debilitate you if you
don't understand who you are and
who you hope to become.

Get to know yourself intricately
and intimately. Find safe spaces
to express yourself freely.

Wear your self-worth like
chainmail. It protects your heart
from the deep wounds of other
people's knives.

With every Breath

let it all go.

Let all their opinions, beliefs, anger, and reactions go.

Let their habits, patterns, facial expressions and disapproving whispers fade like a bird flying away over the distant ocean.

Self-Trust

Self-trust is a superpower. How do
we do obtain this superpower?
We figure out who the FUCK we are
by removing all the voices and all
the lies.
We remove our masks.
We speak up.
We start honoring our heart.
We continuously carve out who we
want to become as we grow and
evolve.
We stay on the path as we paint our
very own beautiful landscape.

As we begin to witness the awe of
our own uniqueness, we learn
self-trust and to never doubt
ourselves again.

You are a masterpiece, and a
masterpiece takes intention and
time. Keep chiseling, climbing,
falling, grasping, inhaling,
exhaling, healing and growing.

Listen and embody your soul's
voice every step of the way.
Your self-worth will find you if you
promise to listen.

Don't abandon yourself. Those who
truly want to love you will see
you. They will honor you and hold
a safe and sacred space for all
parts of you.

If they don't know how to love you,
show them, tell them and ask for
what you need. If they can't, let
them go or you will never be able
to breathe. And you will certainly
never heal.

self-knowing

=

self-honoring

=

self-love

=

self-worth

=

self-trust

=

inner peace

=

personal power

=

Soulful purpose.

Mother & Father

Broken home, abandonment and neglect, and other things I was "shamed" to name.

For my mother & father, the ones who hurt me the most. The mother and father I never wanted to hurt, so I worked tirelessly for decades to be a perfect human – showing up and sacrificing so much, to one day earn your love and gain more than a sliver of your time and affection.

Then I woke up.

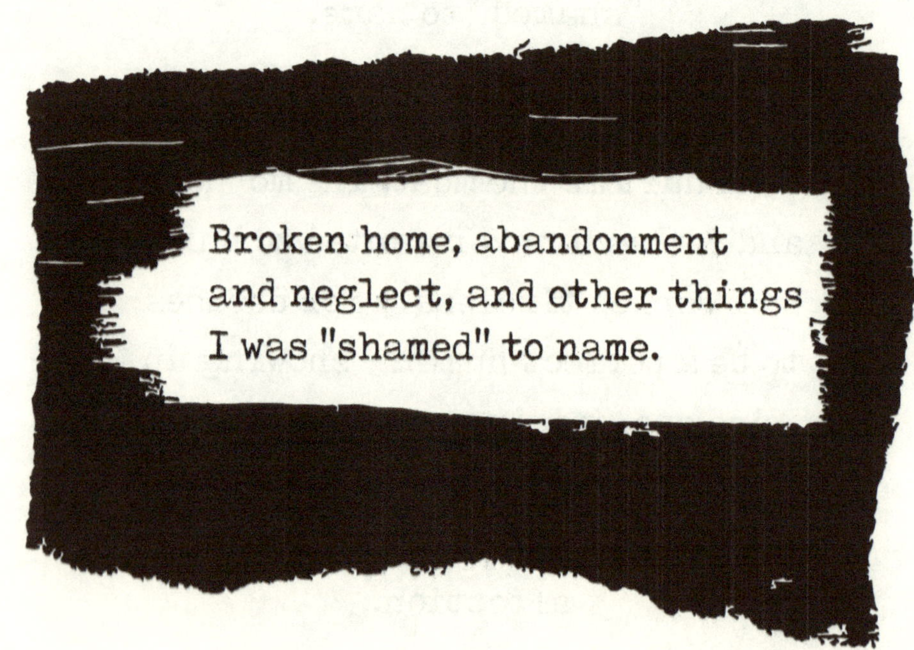

Broken home, abandonment
and neglect, and other things
I was "shamed" to name.

Shame on me.

I never saw my mother and father together, not one single time.

Different worlds, different lives, new friends, new families.

I never saw them talk, hug, hold hands, laugh, or fight. I never saw them cook together or sleep together.

I never sat between them feeling the warmth and safety that my little body and developing brain could recognize as love.

No family vacation, bed-time tuck-ins, side-line cheers, or drying of tears.

No dreams or plans for my future,
or our collective future - or
whatever it is that families do
and dream of...together.

All that was spoken about it was
hatred and regret. No one seemed
to mind this, but I certainly did.
And I was not safe to have a voice
or tears about it.

Shame on me.

Heart-break

Too Much

I was always too much.

If my tears are too much for you,
If you won't sway between the bright
joyful summers and the cold winters of
my life,

If you want only the best parts of me,
but not all of me,

If your heart is void of compassion,

If you refuse to heal,

I'll have to say

Goodbye.

Estranged

I haven't been myself.

I'm grief stricken.

I'd ask for help, but I already know the answer.

It's always been the same.

Instead of re-attempting to explain, or show up for you through my agonizing grief, Instead of pleading and wishing for your understanding, I'd rather suffer alone than feel the anguish of your absence and broken promises - time and time again.

Just going through a period of grief
shut down
lack of energy

Dear Mother,

I was an unwelcomed accident,
so, I was told.
An image of my father,
the man you loathed.
Same skin, same eyes, same...

I was born ugly, born sickly,
born pale and translucent.
You reminded me of this often.
Other family members joined in
the fun.

I smiled and laughed and
pretended. The words and the
stories stay with me, like
invisible poison on my open
wounds.

I can swim

You turned your heart away,
when I was drowning in my angst.

You tethered an anchor to my soul,
didn't try to pull me up,
didn't even come to watch me sink.

My mind filled with fog and fever.
I've been here before, without a
lifejacket, descended and bled
more times than I can count, and
somehow, I still find the strength
to swim.

Dismissed

You had a mother and a father. I
did not. You said you knew you were
loved.

You said I was lucky and told me
you had it worse. Persistently
scorning my pain.

If you had it worse, why do you
continually tell me that you don't
feel the pain I have felt?

I have carried my grandmother's
pain, your denied pain and my pain
in my body and bones all of these
years. Holding it for all of us.
What anguish it has been.

Nurtured

You say there is something wrong with me? I know exactly what it is.

I needed to be nurtured, to be protected, to be seen. Not teased bullied and shamed.

I needed compassion for the chaos, confusion and abuse. The young life I did not ask for.

I needed somewhere to belong.

Voices and Fog

You rejected me for sharing my emotions. For needing to release the pain that wasn't mine to own.

I needed to understand the aching inside my soul - my sadness, my fear and confusion. The constant chaos, loss and uncertainty.

You rejected me for how I looked, dressed, acted, danced, styled my hair. You rejected my choices, my thoughts, my dreams, my voice and my beliefs.

You openly dissected and rejected other women - so I began to reject myself. I was a girl - becoming a woman. You told lies about me. I heard them between the walls.

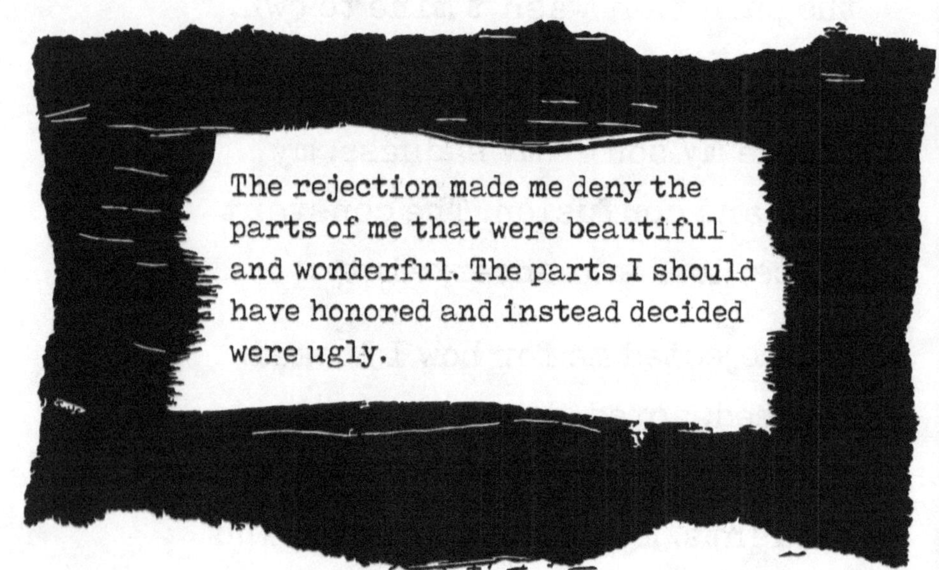
The rejection made me deny the
parts of me that were beautiful
and wonderful. The parts I should
have honored and instead decided
were ugly.

I learned to tell lies to myself - degrading my own beauty and strength.

The rejection made me ashamed of the parts of me that were powerful and intuitive.

The rejection made me hide the whole of me, the human in me, the love in me, the anger in me, the fear in me, the flaws in me, the desire in me, the hunger in me, the beauty in me, the grief in me, the creativity and joyful quirks in me.

My light was always there. I could feel it and see it, but there were too many voices and a dark heavy fog.

Poison

"Is that how you are wearing your hair?"

"Have you gained some weight?"

"Are you going out in public looking like that?"

"Your shorts are too short, you need to wear a bra, put your pants on, no one wants to see that."

"Pull your head out of your ass or I'll knock your teeth down your throat."

"You're a Republican."

"We are christians. You won't be going to heaven if..."

"Stop your whining. Stop your crying. You're too sensitive. No one wants to hear you."

"Life is pain. Suck it up."

"I'll give you something to cry about."

"Don't let the door hit you in the ass on the way out."

"Maybe you are being bullied because you won't keep your mouth shut."

"I brought you into this world, I'll take you out."

"You're lucky I haven't disowned you, after all I've done for you."

"You have issues."

"You're too much."

"Get over yourself."

"There is something seriously wrong with you."

"If you get fat, he will leave you."

Invisible

5 dads, 12+ homes. So many strangers. You said goodbye to them and moved on.

I never could. My heart and memories had a place for everyone. Day after year after decades, sending cards, visiting and delivering gifts.

Showing up and squeezing myself into unwelcome, unfamiliar, and unloving spaces.

New families...just not mine. Hoping to belong.

I didn't. I never understood why.

So, I rejected myself time and time again. **Invisible.**

You do not ask

You assume you know me, but you don't. **You do not ask.** You do not dare or care to see the depths of me.

You misunderstand me because I only exist inside your world, not mine.

I live amidst your desires, your needs, your expectations and your beliefs.

You rarely visit and never stay. Just a minute or two. You have no interest in my home, my life, my heart, my passions or my time.

You do not know me.

Misunderstood

Stop projecting.

Stop protecting.

Stop defending.

Start asking.

Be curious.

Start listening.

Care.

I am not who you think I am.

I never was.

Misunderstood.

Dear Father,

I never knew you. Empty of love, of time or memories. I could only imagine who you might be.

If you knew me, would you see me? Would you love me? Would you want me?

I went for walks outside, rode my bike, sat in the grass, watching and waiting.

Looking for you in the eyes of my teachers and the faces of actors on TV.

I hoped you would walk up to me, and say "Hello, I'm your dad."

I hoped you would hug me, smile at me, tell me stories, watch me play.

You didn't.

I bled

Your family is not mine, and I am not yours.

I never was.

Only my blood was yours.

And I bled.

You never fought for me.

Fight for me

You never fought for me.

You still don't fight for me.

Wasn't that what you were
supposed to do?

Now I know the answer is
unarguably yes.

I had to heal to realize this.

And now I am fighting for myself.

Alone

A child abandoned and left alone
to tend to themselves will never
feel loved or whole.

A child not protected is an adult
rejected, living in fear, shame
and confusion.

An adult unhealed can learn to
perform. They can be and do
anything they like, but they will
exist without inner peace – living
in survival mode, never
embracing, nurturing or trusting
themselves.

A Fake Letter

From my blood parents who should have protected my heart, who chased their desires, started new families and never realized the mess they left behind or the scars they left all over my heart.

Be Free my Child,

I'm sorry I abandoned you. I was ignorant and selfish. You deserved so much more. I am sorry I am still not showing up for you.

I am sorry I did not hold you in your pain, comfort your cries, protect you when you were scared, fight for you when the world was fighting against you, or support you in the way a child deserves.

I am sorry I was distracted and absent, chasing my dreams and things that are of no value in the end. I am sorry for leaving you to hold yourself up and tend to your fragile heart. I am sorry I neglected you.

I'm sorry I was harsh and unkind and made you fearful and responsible for my actions, my words, and my neglect.

My behavior, my anger and my absence should not have been yours to carry, but you did. That was unfair and too much for your innocent heart.

I am still your parent; you are not mine. **It was never your responsibility to carry my burdens, my pain or my choices.** It is not your responsibility to take care of me, fix me, heal me or chase me until I see your value.

I have so much to make up for, but I am busy and selfish, and I have run out of time.

So be free my child. Free the anguish that grips you. Release all the burdens – the voices – that said you were broken, flawed, not good enough and not worthy of our love or our time.

Release the trauma that keeps you up at night.

Create new experiences, as though you are a child once again, and try not to look back.

Bring the people with you that
see you, support you and love you in
the way you always deserved. Keep
them close for they will fill the
void that creeps into your soul
when you think of me.

Let me go child because I cannot be
there for you. Let me go,
because you are worthy, and you
are whole.

~~Respectfully, Warmly,~~

Neglectfully,

Your ~~Mother & Father~~ Blood

revisiting

Trauma

Depression. Grief. Re-Parenting.

Every trauma tells a
lie about who you
truly are.

Dear Trauma,

I'm sorry I refused you. They told me you didn't exist. They told me to give myself away (my gifts, my love, my time) and in doing so, it would take away my pain.

Now I know that by denying you, I was abandoning myself. Shunning myself, carrying the heavy angst with a mask of perpetual joy.

Facing you meant finding myself buried beneath all the lies. Unearthing you meant freeing myself.

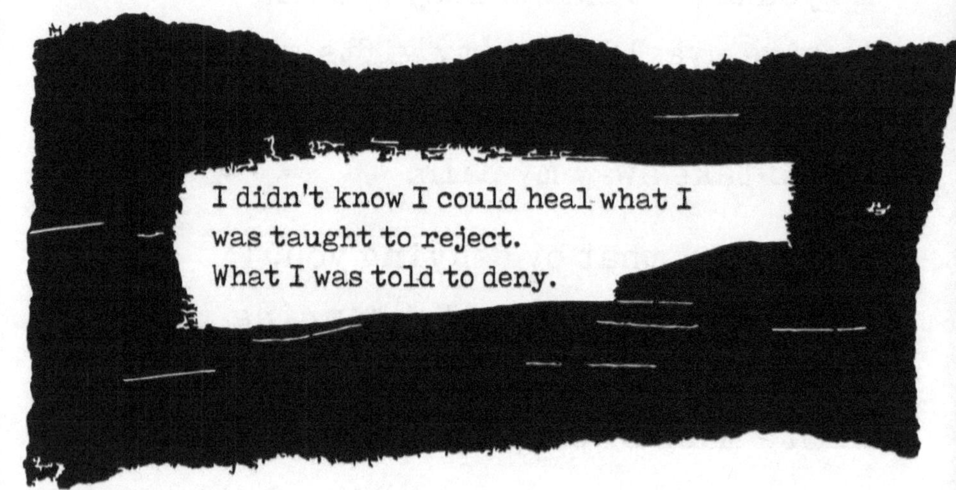
I didn't know I could heal what I
was taught to reject.
What I was told to deny.

Dear Trauma,

I seek to expose you, scrutinize to understand you, confront you when you speak and spoil, and turn the lies you told me about myself into the truth of who I really am.

Trauma Hides

Trauma interrupts pleasure,

it rejects the flow,

it reenacts and mimics.

Trauma is angry,

it shames and lies,

it hides in the shadows,

then appears with a mask.

A guise for every occasion and
every act.

Trauma is not your friend until
you befriend it.

The Ledge

I had it all under control.
My not so perfect life.

The life I crafted and chiseled out
of the need to belong and be loved.

I did not anticipate the fall.
I'm not certain anyone ever does.

Into the Flames

I didn't know I could heal what I
was taught to refuse.

So, pretending led the show, and
perfection took the stage.

I mastered the act and
participated in the tale.

I danced and swayed with sorrow,
as my soul kept calling.

When the embers of expression
turned into a raging fire,

I honored and released the cries
of my soul, and into the flames I
went.

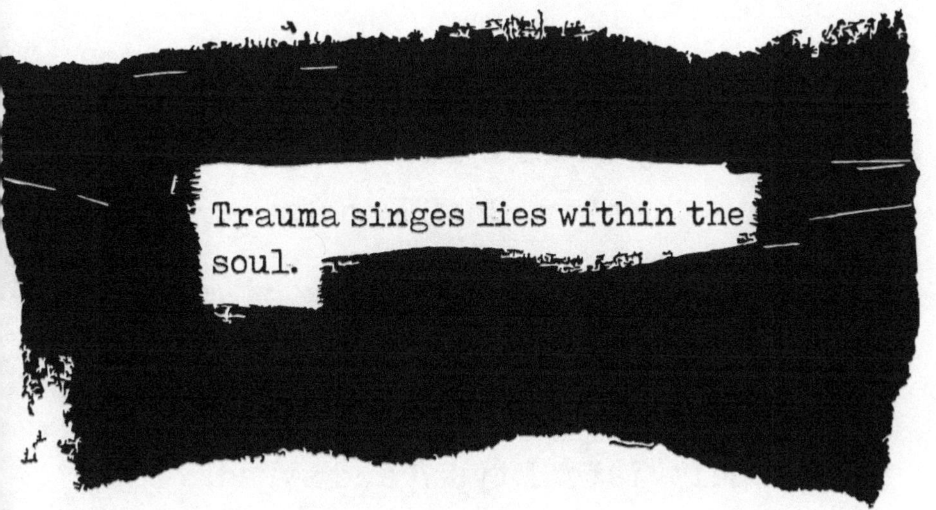
Trauma singes lies within the
soul.

Layers

I typed and cried, slept and suffered.

I began to peel back some thick and sticky layers. The ones that remove the skin. Ones I had never peeled before.

As I read and listened to healing podcasts and popular psychologists, I typed and typed, and the layers of sorrow were erupting then dying and falling off.

It seemed to never end, yet I was seeing things more clearly. The validation of my ambiguous grief. The inaccuracies and truths all appearing from behind the dark

spaces that were enveloping my
heart.

There were days when I would
surface for air only to sink back
down again. Reminding me that I
was still swimming in the middle
of an ocean. Near drowning and
searching for a lifeboat.

My heart was closing in places it
had never closed before. Love
doors shut and locked. Keys thrown
into the abyss, to never be found.

My energy was dwindling, my anger
fighting for the stage, and the
poetry I was bleeding out seemed
to be my only antidote.

The paint I was smearing and
spreading on thick paper gave me
respite.

Unworthy

When unworthy is your belief,

Selfish saves your life.

Silence is Poison

When there is no place to share our pain, we carry it. Many of us carry decades of pain in our bodies – some to the grave. We desperately need to start holding safe spaces for people to feel and be honest. If we want to save lives, the silence must end.

Silence feels like POISON

Fire

There were so many moments I didn't want to feel. This aching, this gnawing, this sadness and fear. I didn't fully honor what was coming up. I tried to avoid it, but I couldn't. It wouldn't let me.

Then, I thought of all the people like me, suffering in silence and shame, and I had to stand up for myself and fight for my wholeness and my worth. I had to save my life, so that others might be able to do the same.

I thought of my kids and the example I would be setting by staying in pain and staying stuck. I thought of my beautiful daughter who couldn't see her worth. Who was giving her heart away to vultures. I thought of my son, who needed my strength, not my weakness.

I knew in the depths of my soul, I had to keep stepping into the flames, as many times as it took.

When you are ready to step into the heat and feel the blisters of your truth. When you are ready for healing, I hope my words will carry you through the fire.

There's no other way around it. You must step through it to get to the other side. You are never alone. There are many others.

Parasite

I recently watched a mini-series called Ptolemy Gray. The lead actor does a good job of portraying how trauma shows up daily, even decades after the events. It shows up unannounced and uninvited in every circumstance of your life. In your conversations, your dreams, in the shower and in your relationships. It is like a parasite that will not die. Remove the parasite.

Shadows

Trauma singes lies within the soul.

Wounds birth the callous or build the kind.

Neglect carries the trauma.

Memory provokes the wounds.

Denial forms the scars.

<u>Extraction of Shadows Poem</u>

1. **Trauma singes lies within the soul.** (You were never good enough. You are unlovable.)

2. **Wounds birth the callous.** (Repeated bullying, name calling, gaslighting, neglect, and abuse creates a need to become a peak of perfection that can never be reached) **or build the kind** (I never wanted anyone to hurt the way I did / do, so I tried my hardest to make everyone happy, to feel loved and seen because I always felt invisible. I felt hated by my mom and other family members and unwanted by my dad because he did not exist. I felt a burden and annoyance to everyone. Rejection was my internal existence. I learned to reject and push people away before they could do it to me. I had to protect myself.

3. **Neglect carries the trauma.** (Spending most of my time alone as a child, no compassion, little kindness, no emotional support, no

acknowledgement, no apology, no ownership, no repair, no healing. Just alone, scared and often confused in the chaos.

4. **Memory provokes and opens the wounds** (Sounds and events, patriarchal traditions and holidays, smells, scenery, repeated and unevolved conversations, dysfunctional patterns, religious programming that caused me internal harm, etc;)

5. **Denial forms the scars** (Bypassing, comparing, ignoring, rejecting, lies, judging, gaslighting). Zero repair or ownership from adults.

Grief

Grief needs a place to be felt,
expressed, seen. It needs support
by the griever and the witnesses.
It needs compassion from
beginning to end - even when it
never fully ceases.

Magnificent Compassion

I could jump off this ship,

sink to the bottom,

closing my eyes,

my mind and my heart,

but I am refusing to bypass my
wounds.

Isolated and undistracted,

I AM weathering the storm,

navigating the harsh waves,

trusting...

staying...

transforming...

into a new human,

embodied with magnificent
compassion.

Shadows of Perfection

All of the emotions it was not okay for me to have. This is where I found my shadows:

Sadness, fear, loneliness, anger, frustration, and crying of any kind. My beliefs or opinions were unwelcome and met with anger, threats and violence.

My objections of circumstances that weren't my choice and out my control, resulting in confusion, chronic instability, and persistent pain.

Being chronically alone and changing schools almost every year caused me to be bullied by peers and family when I wasn't able to handle the events on my own. I was labeled by family as a problem child with issues.

I was gossiped about for the purpose of positioning me to be a flawed person.

I was hurting and my pain was more than justified. But I wasn't allowed to talk about it or feel it.

I was beautiful and wonderful. I wish I had truly known how wonderful I was. It resulted in persistent rejection of myself on every level.

I did not turn to drugs or alcohol. I turned to chronic perfectionism and self-blaming.

I turned into the reliable and consistent giver.

I Grieve

Because it was not repaired, I grieve.

Because I deserved to be heard, I
grieve.

Because my pain was rejected,
I rejected myself,
over and over again.

Because it mattered to me, and I
experienced it, it was real.

Because I still carry it, it still
counts.

Because those who hurt know that
there is no way to fool the knife.

Grief keeps me from falling asleep and
wakes me up in the early hours of the
night.

Because feelings shouldn't need to
hide.

Ambiguous Grief

When I see mothers and fathers holding, embracing, touching, lifting and loving their children, wondering what that would have felt like, and how that would have changed my entire world.

I finally see and trust myself as a mother. I watch as my children feel safe and seen. I watch as they sleep, and they grow. I watch as they cry, laugh, ponder and play. I hold space for them to become who they truly are so they can have a voice, a choice, a place. And my bleeding heart slows to a peaceful beat just for this moment, as I breathe.

As I look back, love intentionally, give freely and tirelessly, I grieve.

And, just for a moment, when I let go of what I so desperately longed for as a little girl, a young woman and a mother, I realize, forever I will grieve.

I accept this knowing and I hold myself
with no shame.

My children are beautiful, wonderful
adults now.

Grief is certain,

it comes at a cost.

it shows up when we choose to feel,

all that we have **lost.**

Grief is certain,

it never knows the score,

it plays the game too many times,

for all that we keep **longing** for.

Letting Go is not easy,

not as simple as a choice,

for the griever always knows,

and only the pain has a **voice.**

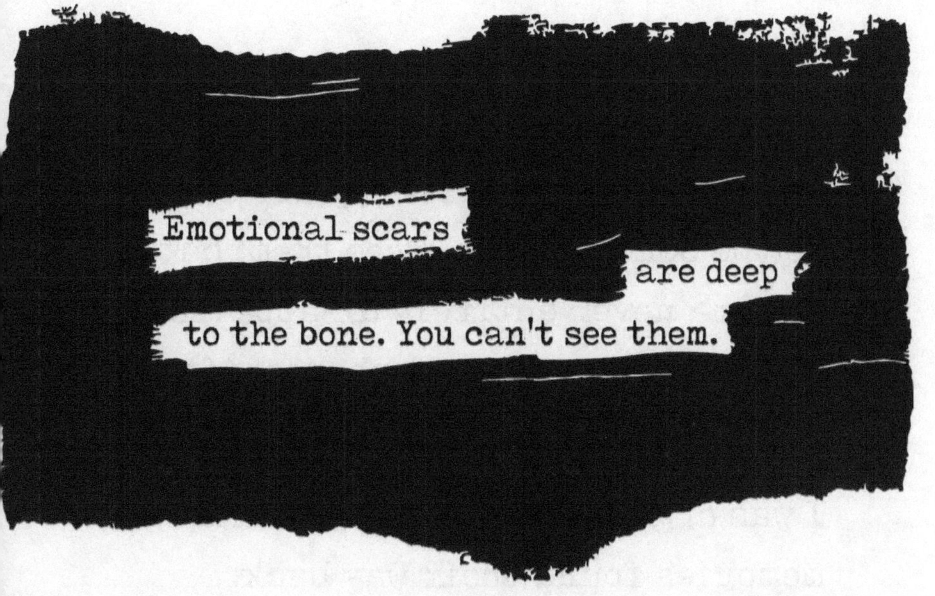
Emotional scars
are deep
to the bone. You can't see them.

Warriors

Today, I put down my sword and wept as I reflected on how hard I've fought for a happy and healed life.

Emotional scars are different than physical scars. They are deep to the bone. You can't see them, but trauma never entirely disappears. It is unsuspecting, it shapeshifts and hides. It always reminds you.

I was organizing photos, and the memories found their way back. The tears were different this time. I'm still grappling with the words. It feels like a rite of passage. Something native, something beautiful.

I reflected on how I feared the

adults in my life and how I was
hell bent on making sure my kids
felt safe, seen, heard and valued.
I had no tools for this. Just
determination and fierce love.

I reflected on how many nights
and decades I cried myself to
sleep. How many personal
sacrifices I made so my kids would
NEVER feel the aching pain and
rejection I felt growing up.

How many times I had to drag
myself out of the dark places
because my little humans were
counting on me to show up and be
everything they ABSOLUTELY
deserved.

I still cry, almost every day. I
have HUGE gratitude and relief
for my strength and fortitude for
cleaning up the messes that were
never mine to own.

For fighting for myself and my kids and my little family.

I will never stop because warriors don't quit. They carry the heavy sword – the sword of the wounded – we are fierce, and we know how to slay!

We are the wounded healers.

Nurtured

Nurtured wounds

transmute into

compassion,

truth,

self-worth,

strength,

wisdom,

wholeness.

Little Me

Younger Me

a Version of Me

No Longer Me

Returning to Me

Take my
hand,
you're
safe.

Cry sweet
child.

I know it feels like you are
drowning. Release the pain or it
will choke you. When your eyes
swell and you cannot breathe,
take a break – sing and dance –
even as the water flows. For this
will lift the heaviness you hold.

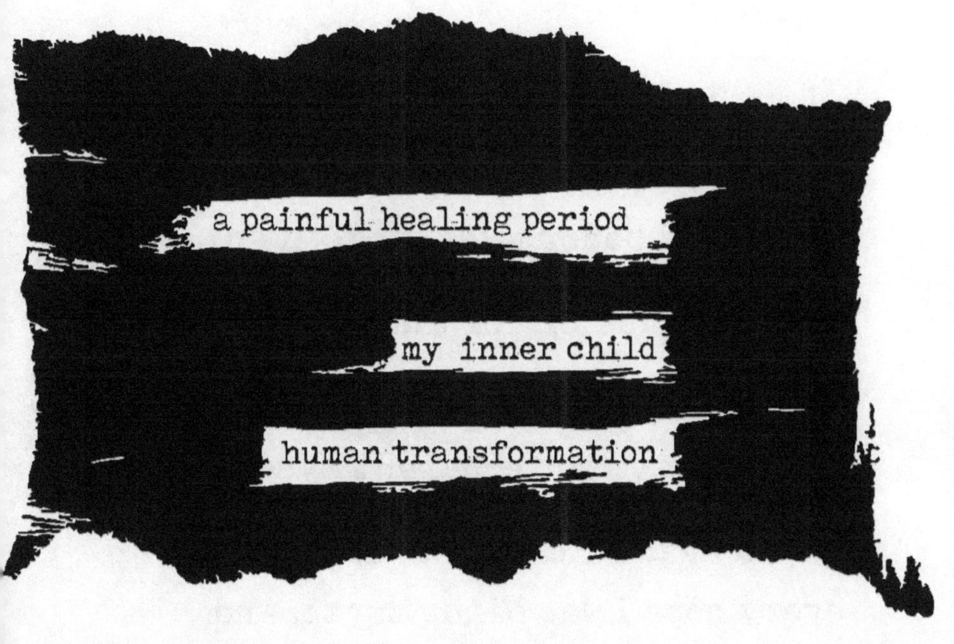
a painful healing period
my inner child
human transformation

If I ever

If I ever wanted to find me,
or BE me...

If I ever wanted to heed the
clarity of my own voice,

trust and honor myself,

have compassion for and dare to
love and nurture myself,

I would have to **re-parent** myself.

Which meant I'd have to let go of
every hope I was clinging to, and
finally say good-bye.

Magical Internal Compass

I dream of a magical compass.

One that I hold safely in my hand,
cupped against my heart.

It leads me through every
emotional maze.

Abandonment made her believe she was flawed.

Neglect made her abandon herself, made her unworthy and invisible.

Unworthiness made her reject herself. Her body, her mind, her feelings, her voice and her power.

Rejection made her sad and lonely, depressed and angry, confused and anguished.

Objectification and insults made her hunt for perfection.

Bullying made her fight for her life and her place in this world.

Denial and Bypassing kept her heart wounded and hemorrhaging.

Religion made her tireless to find her truth, only to uncover lies.

Hypocrisy and lies made her flee.

Pieces of me

I learned to be strong, to survive,
to count on no one. I learned that
independence meant acceptance,
and compassion doesn't exist.

I learned that asking for help was
shameful, and men never stay,
unless you mother them and give
them everything they need. I
learned that sexy and serving is
the golden ticket.

I learned that women are dirty
and flawed, and I must never be
flawed, but yet I was human, from
my very first breath.

I learned if someone gave
me a minute or two, a breadcrumb or
two, a rare hug or thoughtful
word, I was lucky.

I learned that chasing money and
working until my back breaks
will earn me respect and keep me
safe.

I was told that anything good that
happened for me was luck or from
God. The man god, of course. Not
because of me, or because I was
smart and deserved it.

So, I set out on a life's mission
to deserve it.

This exhausted me and broke me
into pieces.

100 Rivers

I've been deeply and fiercely
loving people my entire life.
Everyone – even strangers and
people who didn't know I loved
them – always wanting others to
feel loved – assuming they didn't
feel it and needed mine.

I've been chasing people that
didn't love me back. I kept at it,
because that's what the abandoned
and neglected do. We give so
freely, that which we long for.

I'm all out of love... almost
empty... drained dry.

I've cried 100 rivers and finally
I've opened my heart and my
attention for my younger self, and
the 20, 30, 40+ year old self that
was in survival mode. She's been
waiting.

Now my sweet girl can drink from
the rivers of self-love.

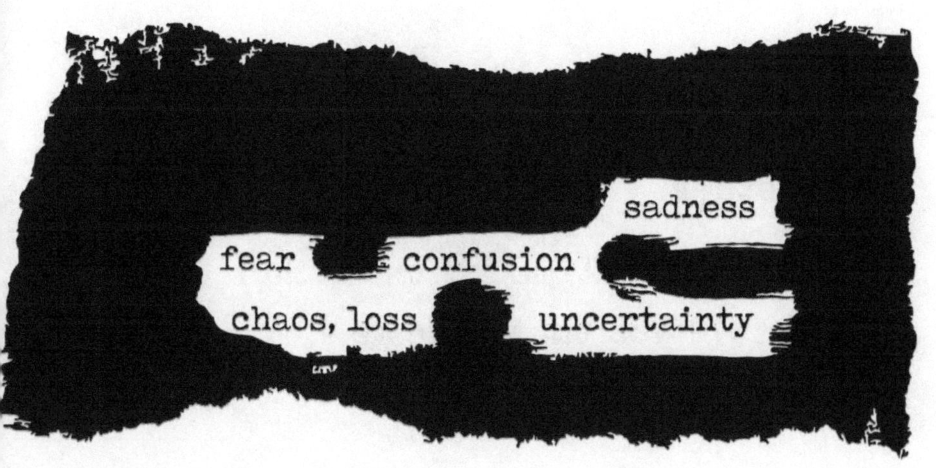
sadness
fear   confusion
chaos, loss   uncertainty

Shame

"Your sadness is drama."

"Your emotions are not welcome here."

"Come back when you have it together."

"There is no time for the human parts of you that make me uncomfortable."

Sadness is ugly.

Sadness is weak.

Sadness is not tolerated.

There are consequences to sadness.

Forgiveness

You don't have to forgive,
What you need to do is accept.
To let go and love yourself the way
you deserve to be loved, because
you will certainly never forget,
and they will never ask or dare to
understand.

When they are ready to repair
what they threw away, they will.

Stop chasing them and stop
abandoning yourself.
Stop rejecting yourself,
Stop shaming and attacking
yourself.

Stop.

STOP
bullying and
abandoning
yourself.

A Letter to Me

Look into my eyes my beautiful child. I see you. I choose you. Forever.

Never be afraid to cry, to feel, to fear, to live. You have been set free.

Now you can fly.

Above all, never lose sight of yourself. You are no longer a problem to fix, but a miracle to discover.

Let's take this journey together anew.

Love,

Me.

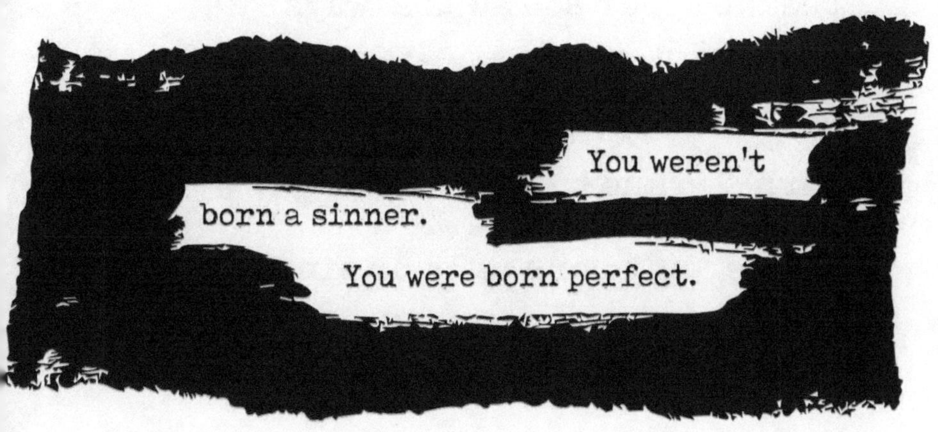
You weren't
born a sinner.
You were born perfect.

I love you little one

pause...silence...discomfort...

awkwardness...

because your soul was always beautiful. You never needed to be saved or changed. You weren't born a sinner.

You weren't born ugly or sinful. You were born perfect. You never needed a rulebook on how to be good.

People broke you because your heart was so big and so pure, your light so bright, your big dreams and hope for all that is humane.

Your fearless and wild heart, your quirky ways and relentless desire for truth made them frightened and uncomfortable.

You scared them because you were different. Because you asked the hard and forbidden questions.

Your desire to see others live their best lives, to be happy, to feel loved and be supported is why I love you.

Because you want the best for others. Because you care about the things that matter... the trees, the animals, the flowers, the earth.

You care about the hearts, minds, and bodies that are happy and healed.

I love you!

The pain and wisdom of being a

Woman

You will never be able to serve,
hustle, perform, sacrifice or
please your way to perfection,
peace, love, or belonging.

Woman

raw
native
true
whole

She

She feared the unknown but faced
it. She dressed like they said she
shouldn't, spoke like they told
her not to, and sang like they said
she couldn't.

She knew very well she would make
people uncomfortable, and both
judgement and gossip were sure to
follow.

But she chose to be brave and free,
and to love herself among humans
who were doing the same.

And the music reached in and
pulled the sadness from her bones.

Speak

The girl in me,
The daughter in me,
The granddaughter in me,
The woman in me,
The mother in me,
My spirit in me,
needs to feel,
and refuses to shrink,
because she must heal.

    .... I must finally heal.
    .... Women, we must heal.

Entangled

No matter how educated, fun, wise, creative, hard-working, witty, or successful you are, you cannot escape your unexamined wounds.

They live in the blood of your organs and the crevices of your body. They take residence in the marrow of your bones, your womb, the depths of your mind and the cries of your soul.

They are entangled within all of you that is pure, true, wonderful, and powerful.

No other way

Surrender the pain and face the truth. There is no other way.

The Pour

I stopped loving people so deeply.

I had to save my life.

I poured so much,

so often,

and my love ran dry.

My earth cracked,

my body collapsed,

my mind yielded,

and my heart stopped.

I grieved, I rested, I learned.

Darkness

I removed my veil and lay naked
with my pain and my truth.

The dark was cold, it left me
scared and alone.

I held firm through the depths,
breathing and surrendering,

Until I emerged to the surface of
my miraculous human
transformation.

The Veil

The veil protects you, yet it takes away your power. It makes you a prisoner. It hides the best parts of you that others never wanted you to see. The parts of you that scared them.

"Remove your veil and put on your crown. You are a Queen."

Follow the rules

Stay skinny

Suffer in silence

Give him a kiss

NO

Fix Your hair,
Wear these clothes,
Lose the weight,
Smile and be nice,
Filter your words,
Follow the rules,
Know your place,
Clean, Cook, Serve,
Have some children,
Stay skinny,
Be grateful,
Don't complain,
Don't cry, don't whine,
Suffer in silence,
No one wants to hear it.
Don't be rude,
Give him a kiss.

What some men say...

Nice ass.

Nice tits.

Girl, I could eat you like a sandwich.

You're a spinner.

I'll show you what it feels like to be a woman.

You are mine.

Women are only good for certain things.

Hot.

A whole lot of nothing.

women are dirty
and flawed

You're Not

You're not
too old.
too young.
too fat
too skinny
too anything...

You're not
too loud,
too much,
too sensitive,
too anything.

You are everything.
You are TOO everything!

BE TOO EVERYTHING.

My Beauty

is in my torn and tattered heart.
My heart that bleeds and beats
among the stitches and scars.

My heart so big and bright, that
only angels and magic can access
it.

Less

The world told me I need to become
more. Consume more. Reach for
more.

My intuition told me I needed less.

...less distractions
...less shallow conversation
...less arguing
...less food
...less trinkets
...less perfection
...less dishonesty
...less poison
...less judgement
...less competition
...LESS!

What do I want?

I don't want to be a woman in a three-piece suit, competing with the rules of the patriarchy, existing only my masculine energy, avoiding the acumen of my human emotions, deaf to understanding and empty of compassion.

Collecting things that make me popular, stroking my ego, running from myself, refusing to face the lies of our collective fears, and feasting on our hunger for endless consumption.

I want the madness to end.

The Portal

Ten years ago, I was young. I looked and acted young. I may still be young. I won't really know until I look back.

I have recently stepped through a portal. I don't recognize parts of myself. Some physical, but mostly the intuitive and lost parts of myself that I have recaptured through the pages. The parts forgotten and rejected along the way. The parts of me that have decided not to take any more meaningless shit from others or myself.

My voice is getting louder, and other people's voices are fading in the distance.

My soul is unshackling itself. I am shedding, peeling, excavating and examining like never before.

The dark clouds are changing into a magnificent spectrum of colors - like a Florida sunset - and the rain is cleansing me.

It is not a baptism; it's a re-birth. The sun is finally breaking through.

My young self and new self are getting acquainted. We are certain to experience more battles, but we are becoming fast friends and loyal companions.

New Realm

This new realm is beyond brilliant.

My intuition is no longer a whisper. It is fierce and powerful.

The portal door is closing behind me, and my previous world is faint in time and space.

I am going to remain here in this new place, until I outgrow it, and prepare to step through the next portal.

The thing about

Getting older

Your body is inviting you to do less. It sends signals if you dare to listen.

Your soul is inviting you to become irrevocably authentic, and compassionately present.

Present for yourself first. Others next.

It takes intuitive wisdom to accept this invitation.

To be a listening human, a curious human, a compassionate human.

Uninhibited

Authenticity is the emotional self, fully expressed. Our instinctual, intuitive, creative, raw, uninhibited human self.

It is native.

You are Woman

Share your raw self,

your native self,

your true self,

your expressive self,

your whole self.

I am Woman

grounded
safe feeling
freedom flow.

Color, laughter,
experiences
emotions self-awareness
life
creating authenticity.

master practice
letting go. give receive,
bend shift
embody wisdom
discernment breath,
presence,
intuitive.
I am everything.
I am WOMAN.

Blooming

I planted new seeds of love in the
cracks of my abandoned heart.

The seeds of nurturance in the
gardens of my own.

I watered my soul and nourished
my mind.

And when my love bloomed again,
I chose myself this time.

Relationships

Everyone has wounds.

Unconscious

We bring our unhealed
generational and personal wounds
to every relationship. We
mindlessly act them out.

We must excavate, examine, own,
and name them. This is how we
heal our bodies and souls. We must
make the unconscious conscious.

This is how we move towards hope
for healthy, happy, safe, secure
and resilient relationships.

99

Until you make the unconscious
conscious, it will direct your life
and you will call it fate.

~Carl Jung

99

Shame lives in silence.

~Brene Brown

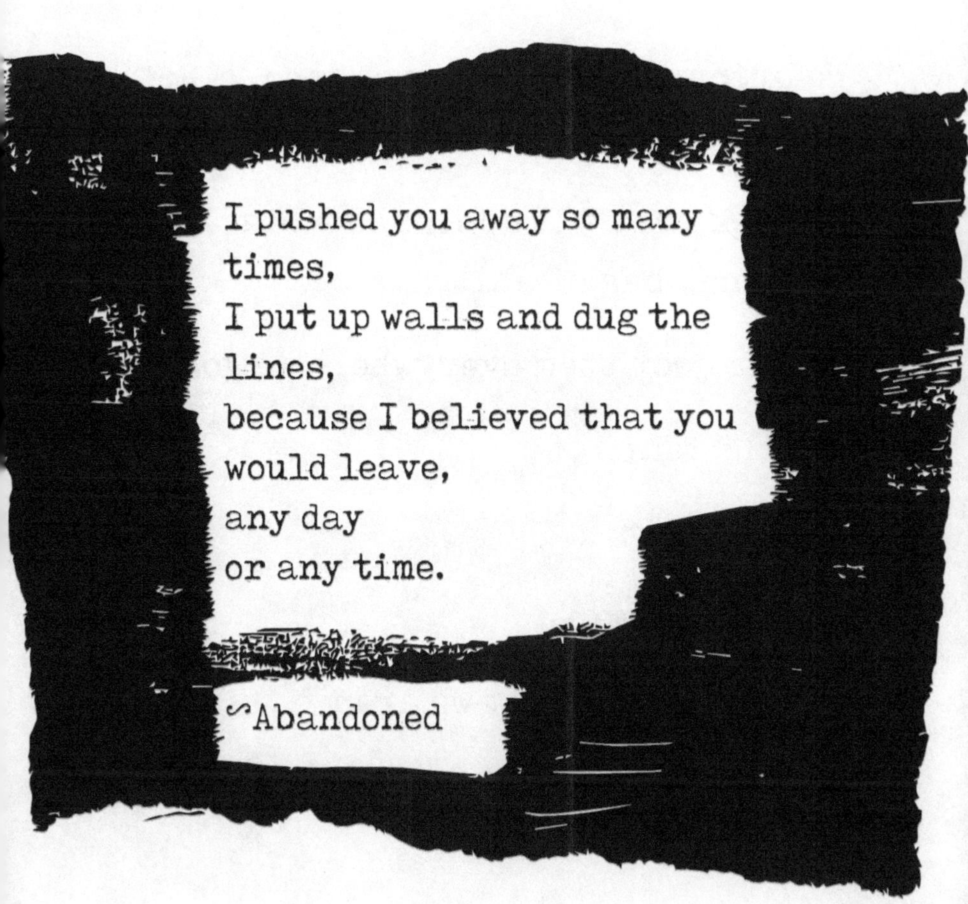
I pushed you away so many
times,
I put up walls and dug the
lines,
because I believed that you
would leave,
any day
or any time.

⌁Abandoned

Projections

We bring them all, every wound,
big or small.

We pack them all up inside a big
internal bag of shit,

and project them everywhere we go.

All the fear,

All the pain,

All the blame,

All the voices that we aren't
enough.

All of it.

Enough

When their best

Is the neglect and abuse,

Is the constant excuse,

Is the bare minimum,

Is broken promises,

Lies and gossip,

Is empty and absent enough.

You reject yourself.

Until you choose yourself.

Eat

Stop accepting crumbs. You do not

need to starve.

End the war you've been fighting

inside.

Feed your body, your mind

and your soul-what it has been

starving for.

The truth of your worth.

The Standard for Love

The standard for love is where
the bar is placed.

I can no longer be

in spaces, environments, the company of, or relationships where I am not allowed to feel deeply and be an emotional human.

Where I can't be honest about what hurts me without ridicule or denial.

Where relationship repair is absent, and humans continue to negate my experiences or take responsibility for their actions.

Where I am misunderstood because no one is curious enough to ask, too busy to care, or too afraid to hear the truth.

Where people choose to make assumptions and gossip over being curious and kind.

Where judgement is the main theme.
Where people watch me behind the
curtain, taking jealousy notes
and stealing my power instead of
lifting me up.

I will no longer allow people to
ignore, reject or dismiss me
because I am different in
thinking or believing.

I will no longer pour into
bottomless pits or spaces where
there is no seed or soil or
reciprocity, and where my ocean of
love feeds into others while it
drains from the rivers and
fountains of my undying love.

I choose to love myself going
forward because I finally realize
that I am worthy.

My voice matters.

My heart matters.

My life matters.

My happiness matters.

My soul belongs to NO ONE,

And I will step into my power
and decide what is best for me.

And that goes with my body too!

Shallows

I never belonged in the shallows.
The deep is where I was always
searching, and where I always
belonged.

Eroding

If you can't talk about what pains
you with the person who is hurting
you, the relationship will die
on the festering surface,
shallow,
empty,
burning,
stuck,
stale,
and meaningless.
Eventually eroding
into dirt and dust.

Curiosity

Curiosity invites.

Honesty allows.

Transparency opens.

Compassion cures.

Understanding deepens.

Safety holds.

Trust builds.

Transmutation begins.

Healing begins.

People unafraid of depth and vulnerability are my kind of people.

Tribe

My Kind of People...

Awkward, quirky, kind, silly healing, authentic people are my kind of humans.

People unafraid of depth and vulnerability are my kind of people.

Funny people with BIG hearts and unbelievable stories that are sacred and true. Stories that choke you up, change your heart and open your mind.

People with multi-dimensional souls colored with endless compassion who see the broken and feel the pain and want to help mend it – those are my kind of people.

We must deepen
the roots in
the soil of our
relationships.

The Soil

My desire to be open about my feelings and experiences – of what has hurt or harmed me is not negativity. **It is not living in the past.** It is being present and honest with my pain and **returning to the places that have the answers.**

It is unearthing, it is self-learning, self-understanding and self-awareness.

It is a heroic act of self-love. A willingness of vulnerability and truth. It is a deep desire to practice honesty with others and myself. To transmute pain into wholeness and **deepen the roots in the soil of my relationships.**

Walls & Lines

I pushed you away so many times,

I put up walls and dug the lines,

because I believed that you would leave,

any day or any time.

~Abandoned.

Keep the humans that don't abandon you in your grief.

For, they are rare.

Those who dare.

Those who dare to understand the vast expressions of love, (including grief) will not abandon you.

They can both bathe in your joy and put down their sword to hold your wounds with quiet tenderness.

he sees me . . . . He loves me

because I cry, because I am not afraid to feel what many humans forbid. He loves me because of the way I wear my heart - torn wide open for everything to bleed and pour out.

He says I give him strength - I inspire him- I am brave. He admires my courage to be seen, to take risks, to be embarrassed, laughed at and misunderstood - even when it hurts.

He acknowledges my female sacrifices. The surrender of ego and pride, body, flesh, and selflessness for the whole. He sees me because I asked him to, and he was finally willing, when I said I had to go.

When you fall . . .

When you fall, I'll pick you up.

When you can't walk, I will carry you.

When you hurt, I won't turn my back on you.

When you decide to change, I'll support your growth.

When we don't agree, I will still love you.

When your vision is blurred, I'll help you see.

When your heart aches, I'll plant a seed.

When you can't find the words, I'll help you speak.

When you forget, I will remind you.

My New Wedding Vows

Husband Steadfast

and grounded. **You made my dream of a family with "two parents and their kids" come true.**

We unsuspectingly wounded each other along the way. We brought all of our unhealed pain and anger to the playground of life. We didn't even know it and didn't have the tools, but we had the love, and we are doing the work.

You are my best friend. Thank you for making it to the other side of this transformation with me. I am forever grateful, and we are finally learning what love should feel like.

Thank you for holding my hands,
rubbing my aching body, the love
notes in the morning, touching me
when I didn't know what it felt
like to be touched, listening to my
endless cries, wiping the rivers
of tears from my mascara-
streaked cheeks and looking
into my eyes when I never felt seen.

Thank you for not abandoning me
in my pain. Thank for being
willing to grow and change.

187

A Poet's Playground

De-Construction

Losing Religion & Saving my Soul

Spiritual Predator

Someone who tries to manipulate your spiritual journey, bypass your pain with scripture and prayer, and control the outcome of your soul.

My soul is not for sale

Vultures are always circling

My Soul

is not for sale,

it is not for bargaining or
debate.

Vultures are always circling.

Intuition

The voice.

The whisper.

The nudge.

The self-knowing and self-trust.

The gatekeeper of my soul.

Chokehold

Let go believer. The chokehold

you have on your firm beliefs is

suffocating you and those you love.

It is separating all that

connects us. When you let go of

the certainty and absolutes, you will

begin to take in tiny breaths of

truth and life.

Fear

Keep your fears and your scriptures to yourself.

I am not what you told me, not who you said I must be.

Your beliefs are no longer mine to carry. Your wounds are not mine to heal.

My truth is not your lie, and I am not yours to convince.

My soul belongs to me. It is not yours to bully, provoke, or condemn.

Religious Mission Statement:

Judgement.
Condemnation.
Rejection.
Hypocrisy.
Gaslighting.
Oppression.
Control.
Manipulation.
Brainwashing.
Lying.
Sexual Misconduct.
Fear.
Loss of self...

all for a small fee of 10% and
losing your intuition and soul.

Bonus: False Promise of Eternity

My religion is

Writing, Poetry,
Painting, Dancing,
Inhaling, Exhaling,
Singing, Floating,
Soaking up the sun,
Breathing amongst the trees,
Earthing in the sand and soil,
And howling at the moon.

I've haven't actually howled at
the moon...yet. Let's do it
together, shall we?

My spiritual practice is
Compassion
and it always
begins
with
myself.

History I prefer to learn

concealed history. The untold stories of suffering and hideous injustice. I can and I have.

I've examined my own history. The suffering and dysfunction. The toxic silent pain.

It ripples down from history to humans, from war to man, then woman to child, then animal to earth. We keep passing down the shrapnel of our wars. The lunacy and the pain. The ceaseless violence and hunger for power and money.

If we intend to survive and truly live, we must be present. We must look within and reunite as one. Collective healing is the only thing that will save us.

We must leave the toxic blood-soaked soil and hate behind.

Jesus didn't save me.

Writing saved me,
after it flayed me.

Jesus didn't save me.
I saved me,
by freeing my soul,
and giving it a voice.

Jesus didn't save me,
my aunt's presence saved me,
a loyal man saved me,
my children saved me,
compassion saved me,
self-love saved me.

Women are not free.

Sinful and dirty,

pretending,

shrinking,

submitting.

Quiet and likeable.

Survival is key.

Women are not free.

God is a Woman

I found my worth,
and this time...
I decided to fall...
madly in love with me.

Not Him.

I AM

Worthy, because I AM, not because someone says I am.

Grateful, because I finally found myself outside of others.

Brave because I refused to fit-in and conform to the destructive broken systems.

All I had to do was look and there I was. Raw, powerful, and wise – a beautiful worthy woman.

Recipe for removing

expired and damaging belief systems and damaging human patterns...

Extract.

Peel.

Discard.

Replace.

Rest.

Create.

Repeat.

Easier said than done, which is why I go into a bit more detail of my personal experience on the following pages.

EXTRACTING

requires a deep commitment to introspection. Extracting and peeling work together. **Extract, Peel, Repeat!**

Peeling sounds painful because it is. Imagine peeling your skin off. That's what removing the brainwashing feels like. Peeling involves raw honesty with your inner examination. It means acknowledging everything that is not serving the highest level of your soul – your spirit and heart.

This type of honesty causes extreme discomfort because it means searching DEEP inside and listening. Intuition speaks.

Distractions or excuses are not viable during the extracting and peeling process. They only delay it and leave the skin hanging.

Learning how to soothe the
nervous system and having access
to safe spaces is crucial when
extracting and peeling.

DISCARDING takes

courage to a whole new level. We are figuratively discarding the dead skin - the unhealthy cells.

It is cleaning the slate. It is accessing the superpower of self-trust and daring to let go of everything you've been clinging onto, including the fear.

Learning to trust and learning to let go take brave and consistent practice. Fear and trust do not work together. Pick trust.

**Self-Trust
is a superpower.**

REPLACING

This is both arduous and fun. It is akin to starting something new and not having any idea what you are doing. Self-trust works with replacing, so hang on to your self-trust. Replacing old programming, beliefs, and old language is an intricate recipe of flexibility, openness, surrender, curiosity intention, and commitment. It will exhaust you. It requires energy and rest.

It takes time because you are researching, learning and practicing a new way of thinking, living, BE-ing and speaking.

Make room for your authentic self in this stage. **Curiosity SUPPORTS replacing.** Be curious and stay curious. Be open and make room for everything.

REST seems simple enough, right?

Some people live an entire life not knowing how to rest. If this is YOU, I urge you to put this on the top of your "replacing" list. And, to be clear, I'm not talking about napping for 30 minutes or working 10 hours instead of 12. I'm talking about a life-saving sabbatical.

Commit to researching books on self-care and rest. Everyone will choose to rest differently, but for the sake of your healing and joyful soul, please learn how to rest.

CREATE This is the
spiritual part of us. The part
where we tap into the youthful
curiosity and the parts of our
heart that needs to express
itself. Art, music, poetry,
forming, fishing, and fixing.
Creating is healing food for the soul.

REPEAT means never
quitting or giving-up because
change is hard, and life is full of
storms. With self-love (nurturing
and rest), we can always find the
shore.

Grace and self-compassion are a
crucial and integral part of the
entire process.

Peace

is when you don't fear death or
eternal burning.

People just want to exploit
and profit from our collective
fears and some just want to be
right.

Live now before it's too late.

Children

Protecting their hearts, their
bodies and their minds.

Young Mother

Keep your heart on the WHY dear mother. I know you are tired and weary. I know you feel invisible.

You are protecting their hearts and healing their future.

You are more crucial than the world dares to recognize. You are leading the way, a lighthouse for all the ships who will sail the erratic seas.

You are building their future, your future, re-writing and repairing the past. You are protecting and nourishing the family you've always dreamed about. Don't give up.

Protect them

Protect her heart, protect his too. Feed them kindness and patience, presence and time. If you do, it comes back to you and heals the past.

Support them with your open heart and healing, not your wounded beliefs or your visions of who they should be. Set your ego aside and dance with them, play with them, laugh and sing with them.

Your presence is a gift. Watch them quietly and closely and you will begin to see the truth of who they are. Soon you will understand when they are not themselves. Help them see themselves because they won't. Not right away.

Show them their gifts, their power, and help them find their voice - they deserve it. Free them from your control and they will show up for you with the most beautiful love.

Give them your absolute best, nothing less, and they will grow and blossom into who they are meant to be.

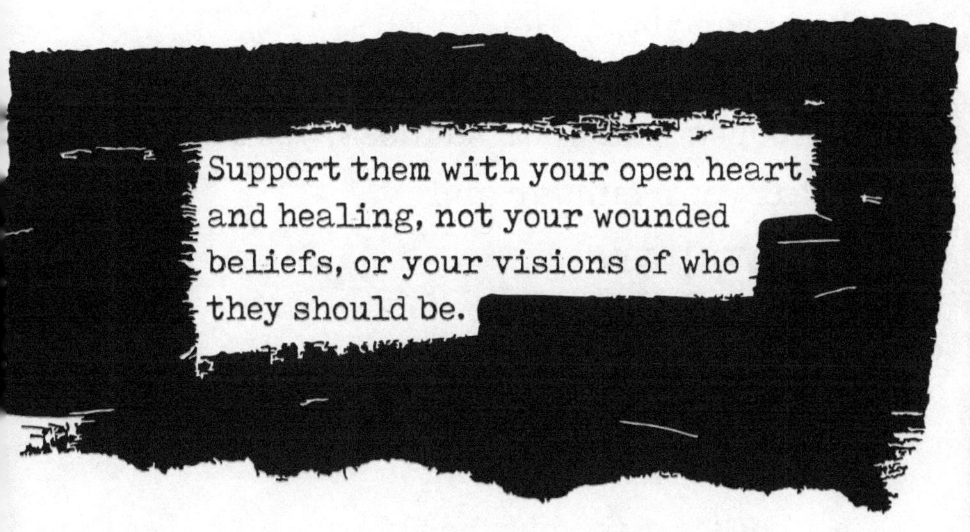
Support them with your open heart
and healing, not your wounded
beliefs, or your visions of who
they should be.

Enmeshed

Your dreams are mine.
What you desire, I imagine and
hope for you.

My bones feel your sadness, your
fear, your hunger and
uncertainty.

My heart opens and my love pours
for you.

My healing is your healing.
Your joy brings me hope.
Your laughter feeds my soul.
Your heart is my why.

I practice patience and self-love
for you.

I laugh and dance for you.

I create space for all parts of
you. I won't deny your experiences,
your pain, your joy, your voice
or your memories.

I see your gifts, and I want you to
see them. Your humanness is
beautiful. I promise to shine only
light and compassion on all parts
of you, so that you never see
yourself as unworthy.

When I'm gone, my hope is that my
love, healing, and my presence for
your miraculous life will stay
with you as you finish your
journey.

You have been nothing less than a
precious gift to every decade of
my life.

Unconditional

Show your children at every age and every stage of life that they can come to you with their pain.

Let them express their emotions and share their experiences without shame, distraction, punishment, defensiveness, rejection, judgement or debate.

Hold a safe and supportive space for every part of who they are.

To my children

Chase & Cheyenne, my best friends.
Our 27 years together and the
gifts you have brought to my life
and my healing are priceless.

To be your mother is the greatest
gift I could **NEVER** have imagined
- until it all came true.

I will forever be your mother,
even after I leave this earth and
travel to another realm.

Come find me when you get there.
I'll be waiting.

Breaking cycles is hard and
lonely work. It is a commitment of
self-sacrifice, letting go, grief,
growth, and hoping you can breathe
again.

Healer
Shadow Slayer

Healer

Cycle Breaker

Fire Walker

Shadow Slayer

Wave Maker

Boundary Layer

Trail Blazer

Path Paver

Live Saver

Wings

Becoming the most beautiful and soulful embodied version of yourself doesn't just happen.

Sure, you can let life happen to you. That's not always the worst thing.

But unwavering dedication to who you become gives you wings.

Who doesn't want wings?

Unchanged

You can't heal if you won't feel.

You won't grow

if you refuse to know,

what it is

or what it was

that wounded your heart,

and denied your soul.

You will stay blind,

deaf,

dumb,

and safe.

You'll remain the same.

Unmoved and unchanged.

Creative Expression

is where perfection ends,

and authenticity begins.

Wildflowers

Give your wounds a canvas.

an infinite landscape

with color, depth, and dimension.

With death and new life.

Let the ache be hot and harsh,

the grief cold and bitter.

Then invite your wounds

to the affectionate climate

of an open valley

blanketed in the trust

of the warm sun

and the limitless wildflowers.

From Sun to Moon

I am shedding what shackles me...

Re-igniting the fire in me...

Searching for what inspires me...

Unearthing what was denied in me...

Revealing only the truth in me...

Unmasking the lies in me...

Examining fear in me...

My natural gifts, my intuitive
wisdom,

my feminine power.

My flame that burns,

from sun to moon.

I would be *free* to think, to

speak, to cry,
to be spontaneously creative,
shifting and flowing,
trusting with ease and calm.
I would welcome my storms,
bending like a wise tree,
hugging and gripping the earth.

I would brave the sullen ocean,
trusting the beckoning waves -
like the open arms of a loyal lover
or faithful friend.

I would float to the shore,
knowing it is there, where I will
rest and then fly once again.

I Am

I am a feminine and masculine
woman, living in the power of my
intuition.

I am healing the shared trauma,
with the grounded strength
of my wise soul.

I am nourishing my spirit with
the presence of my grace and
compassion.

Healers do not

prescribe medicine.

Healers heal others by the relentless offering of compassion.

We sit with the broken in their darkest places,

because we too have been broken – without hope.

Hope is where the seed of life (love) is planted,

and the miracle of healing begins.

You know what is *magic?*

Self-compassion is magic. It is the antidote to self-betrayal.

Self-awareness is magic. It's relentlessly relationship intentional. It sees, hears and analyzes oneself clearly to avoid hurting oneself and others.

Honesty is magic. It is the authentic truth of all that needs to be felt and faced.

Presence is magic. It is energy. It can hold space for deep healing. It is an antidote for abandonment and loneliness.

Listening is magic. It is quiet and peaceful. It is simply curious, seeking only to understand.

Void of judgement or fixing,
listening is healing and
transformative.

It turns "Hear me, see me" into "I
see you, I value you."

It turns "I matter" into "You
matter."

It works miracles alongside
presence.

isms

I put myself in the shoes of the
other.

Which means I agree with
everyone, and I agree with
no one.

We must see ourselves in every
human,

for that is where love begins
and the "isms" end.

Like a *Gardener*

I want to plant, grow and nourish
the hurting humans around me
with the power of my compassion
and presence.

I want to repair the damage of
fear, hate, violence and war,
by breaking cycles,
forging new paths,
and saving lives,
starting with my own.

I want the light of my heart
and the fire of my soul
to transform humanity
like a ray of sun
that has found its way
into the dark and dying spaces.

Every Healer is a *Poet,*

Whether they know it,

share it,

claim it.

When you face it,

and feel it,

You can heal it.

Be a poet.

I love this *Woman*

She is ME. My very best friend. I have lived with her every minute of every hour of every year of her entire life.

She is a fighter. She has fought for her safety, her healing, her life, her feelings, her children, her relationships, her marriage, her soul-sisters, boys and men, her truth and her voice.

She will keep fighting the fight for anyone who can't find their voice. This woman has chosen the heroines journey, a soul-freeing rebirth (or two) and plunged bravely into dark and lonely human transformations.

She's not afraid to get angry, cry, dance, or laugh out loud. She will not be silenced, and she will never abandon herself.

She is woman, she is Virgo, she is Earth.

"We must take refuge in the safety
of healing humans."

Soul Sisters

My beautiful Cheyenne, Tiffany, Sarah, Linda, Yolanda, Julie, Lisa, and my precious Kimberly, who is in another realm - I'm sorry I couldn't heal your pain. I wish I knew back then what I know now.

Thank you for not flinching or judging when I get angry, cry or grieve. For not deserting me as I de-construct, peel, shed, change and evolve.

Thank you from the bottom of my stitched-up heart.

~~The End~~

It took me a couple of years to
finish this book. I can read it now
without crying (mostly) and
without my gut turning and
twisting. Without shame or fear.
Without needing to nap for
several hours (or days) between
edits.

I am different now.
I have given respite to my soul.
I am not living in chronic angst.
I am finding inner peace.
I am worthy without question,
I am compassionate with myself.
I am love.

I always was!

@cheydrea

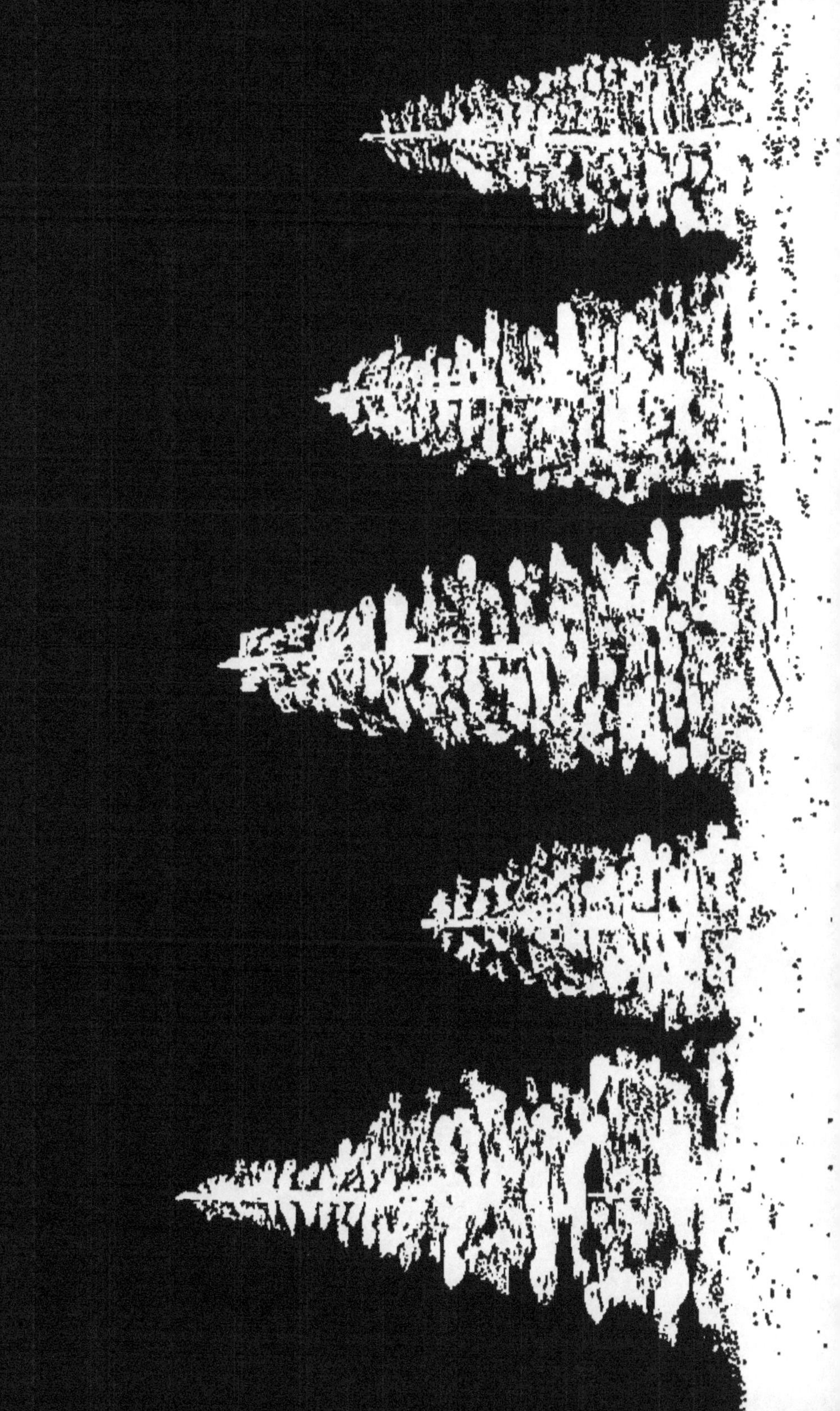